The Adventures of
ULYSSES

Bruce LaFontaine

DOVER PUBLICATIONS, INC.
Mineola, New York

ABOUT THE AUTHOR

BRUCE LAFONTAINE is the writer and illustrator of 48 published books for both children and adults. His nonfiction books are focused within the areas of history, science, transportation, and architecture. His works include *Warriors Through the Ages, Classic Sports Cars,* and *Famous Buildings of Frank Lloyd Wright,* among others. His book *Motorcycles* (1995) received the MVP Award from the American Motorcyclist Association. He is included in *Something About the Author* and the *International Biographical Centre Who's Who of Authors,* hardcover publications profiling prominent authors and illustrators. He lives and works in the Rochester, New York, area.

NOTE

The Adventures of Ulysses is based on the epic poem the *Odyssey,* thought to have been written by the Greek poet Homer in the eighth century B.C. (although scholars are not absolutely sure when Homer lived, or even if he was just one person). A companion to Homer's earlier poem the *Iliad,* which told the story of a ten-year-long war between the Greek city-states and the city of Troy, the *Odyssey* begins at the end of the Trojan War. It describes the arduous voyage home of Odysseus, one of the greatest Greek warriors. Both poems concern events that are believed to have taken place in the thirteenth century B.C. Today, the *Iliad* and *Odyssey* are considered among the greatest works of Western literature.

As mentioned above, the *Odyssey* focuses on a wily Greek warrior-king named Odysseus (the Romans later changed the hero's name to Ulysses, which is the name more widely known to the public and the one used in this book). After the fall of Troy, Ulysses sets out on the return voyage to his island kingdom of Ithaca. As it turns out, the trip takes ten years—as long as the Trojan War itself. During the voyage, Ulysses and his men encounter many obstacles as the hero struggles to get back to his homeland and rejoin his beloved wife Penelope and young son Telemachus. In confronting these challenges, Ulysses relies on cunning and intelligence to prevail, rather than brute force. He is shown to be a complex, flawed, and very human hero.

The *Odyssey* contains all the ingredients of high adventure: heroic deeds, terrible monsters, betrayal, revenge, and exotic characters and locations. *The Adventures of Ulysses* is an illustrated narrative version that faithfully recounts many of Ulysses' famous encounters with mythical beings and strange and unusual creatures. But perhaps its most compelling element is Ulysses' driving perseverance to return to his homeland and faithful wife, which still strikes a universal chord in the human heart.

Bibliographical Note

The Adventures of Ulysses is a new work, first published by Dover Publications, Inc., in 2004.

DOVER *Pictorial Archive* SERIES

This book belongs to the Dover Pictorial Archive Series. You may use the designs and illustrations for graphics and crafts applications, free and without special permission, provided that you include no more than four in the same publication or project. (For permission for additional use, please write to Permissions Department, Dover Publications, Inc., 31 East 2nd Street, Mineola, N.Y. 11501.)

However, republication or reproduction of any illustration by any other graphic service, whether it be in a book or in any other design resource, is strictly prohibited.

International Standard Book Number: 0-486-43328-5

Manufactured in the United States of America
Dover Publications, Inc., 31 East 2nd Street, Mineola, N.Y. 11501

1. The youthful Ulysses is wounded by a wild boar.

As a boy, Ulysses loved to roam the forests and rocky hills of his native island Ithaca, off the coast of Greece. As he grew to manhood, he became a skilled hunter and expert archer. He used a special bow so difficult to draw that only Ulysses himself could string and nock an arrow in the powerful weapon. It was said that his marksmanship was so accurate that he could cleanly shoot an arrow through the openings in twelve aligned axeheads.

One day, during a hunt for the dangerous wild boar that lived on the island, Ulysses suffered a serious leg wound. The wound eventually healed, thanks to the ministrations of his faithful childhood nurse Eurycleia, but it left a ragged scar above his knee. This mark would later figure in the story of the adventures of Ulysses called the *Odyssey*.

2. Ulysses and Penelope, King and Queen of Ithaca.

Ulysses grew up as the son of King Laertes and Queen Anticleia, rulers of the island kingdom of Ithaca. When Laertes grew too old and feeble to rule, Ulysses inherited the throne.

Seeking his own wife and queen, Ulysses traveled to Sparta along with many other Greek kings to ask for the hand of Helen, the most beautiful woman in Greece.

Helen's father Tyndareus eventually chose King Menelaus of Sparta to be Helen's husband. While in Sparta, however, Ulysses met Penelope, niece of Tyndareus, and fell in love with her. She returned his affection and accepted his hand in marriage. Ulysses and Penelope returned to Ithaca to rule as king and queen. Ulysses was overjoyed when Penelope gave birth to a son, Telemachus.

3. Ulysses leaves for the Trojan War.

When Tyndareus chose Menelaus as Helen's husband (see previous caption), there was great resentment and jealousy among Helen's other suitors. One of these suitors was Paris, prince of the city of Troy. In order to maintain peace among the suitors, Helen's father had each swear an oath. If any one of them should take Helen away from Menelaus, all the others would unite against the interloper.

Paris eventually broke his oath, abducting Helen and bringing her back to Troy with him. As a result, King Agamemnon declared war against the Trojans and called upon the other Greek kings to uphold their oaths. The kings agreed, and soon the Greek states had assembled a great fleet and army for the purpose of attacking Troy.

Commanding a flotilla of twelve ships and 600 soldiers, Ulysses prepared to depart, reluctantly bidding farewell to his beloved Penelope and young son Telemachus.

4. Ulysses fights in the ten-year-long Trojan War.

The Greek army assembled to fight the Trojans included many great heroes, but the greatest Greek warrior of all was Achilles. He was the son of Thetis, a sea nymph. As an infant, Achilles was dipped into the River Styx by his mother in order to give him godlike invulnerability. She held him by the heel, making that spot his only weakness.

The Greeks and Trojans fought many battles on the plains of Troy. As the years passed, the war became a stalemate. Finally, Achilles killed the Trojan champion Hector. Soon after that, Achilles himself was mortally wounded in the heel by a poisoned arrow shot by Paris. As the war continued to drag on, a new plan was needed to achieve a Greek victory. In the course of the conflict, Ulysses had distinguished himself as a brave and resourceful warrior in numerous battles. Now, it was he that devised the ingenious scheme that finally won the war.

5. Ulysses devises the plan for the Trojan Horse.

Ulysses came up with the idea of constructing a giant wooden horse capable of concealing Greek soldiers inside. When the horse was ready, the Greeks rolled it, during the night, onto the plain facing Troy. Then the Greek fleet sailed a few miles down the coast, anchoring in a remote cove.

The following morning, the Trojans discovered the giant horse standing on the plain and the Greek camp deserted. They decided that the Greeks had given up the fight, left the horse as a gift for Athena, and then sailed for their homeland. The delighted Trojans brought the horse into the city and began a wild celebration. After midnight, when the Trojan guards were drunk and asleep, fifty Greek soldiers quietly descended from the belly of the horse. Quickly killing the guards, they opened the gates to the waiting Greek army that had returned during the night.

Completely caught by surprise, the Trojans were easy prey for the Greek warriors, who killed the Trojan soldiers and captured their women and children as slaves. Then the Greeks burned the great city, leaving only an empty shell encircled by the huge walls.

6. Ulysses sails from Troy for Ithaca.

After ten years, the siege of Troy had finally ended. At last, Ulysses, the reluctant warrior, could return to his island kingdom of Ithaca and rejoin his beloved Penelope.

Sailing from Troy in a fleet of twelve ships, Ulysses and his men ventured into the Mediterranean bound for home. Unbeknownst to them, many terrifying, tragic adventures lay ahead. Indeed, it would be another ten long years before Ulysses would see Penelope and Telemachus.

7. Ulysses and the Island of the Lotus Eaters.

The fleet sailed west but was soon caught in a fierce storm that blew them far off course. After many days, they reached landfall at the Island of the Lotus Eaters. Here they encountered a group of friendly inhabitants who offered some of the crew fruit from the lotus plant. This fruit had a hypnotic druglike effect on the men, causing them to lose all interest in returning home. Ulysses, realizing that his men would eventually be trapped in a dreamlike state by the lotus eaters, forced the befuddled crew members back onto the ships and quickly set sail.

8. Ulysses and the cyclops.

On their continuing voyage Ulysses' ship became separated from the others in the fleet, and soon ran short of food and water. Luckily, the ship reached an island teeming with sheep and goats. The crew quickly had fresh meat roasting on their fires. Ulysses and a dozen of his men ventured inland to explore the island further.

Coming upon a cave, they found it empty save for a pile of bones. While the men were inside, the light from the cave mouth was suddenly blocked. Standing before them was a giant one-eyed wild man—Polyphemus the cyclops. Son of Poseidon, god of the sea, and a nymph, he lived on the island herding his flocks of sheep and goats. Angry that intruders had eaten his animals and entered his abode, Polyphemus rolled a giant rock in front of the cave mouth, sealing it tightly. Ulysses and his men were trapped!

9. Ulysses and his men blind the cyclops.

Suddenly, Polyphemus grabbed two members of the crew, tore them to pieces and ate them, much to the horror of the trapped Greeks. Ulysses racked his brains to devise a plan that would allow him and his men to escape. At first he thought he might creep up on the monster as Polyphemus lay sleeping and kill him with his sword. But then the Greeks would be trapped forever in the cave, the giant rock door far too heavy for them to move.

Before long, the creature devoured two more of Ulysses' men. In a stroke of good fortune, however, the crew had brought a potent wine with them. They now offered it to Polyphemus, who soon became drowsy from the effects of the wine and fell asleep. Searching through the cave, the Greeks found a stout shaft of olive wood. They sharpened one end, hardened it in the fire, and jabbed the red-hot spear into the cyclops' single eye.

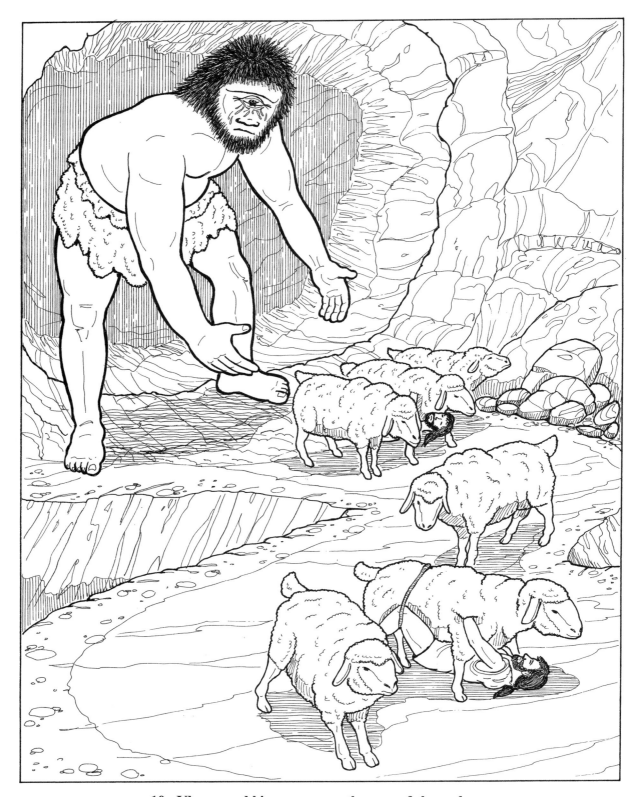

10. Ulysses and his men escape the cave of the cyclops.

Howling with pain and rage, the blinded cyclops scoured the cave for the Greeks, but could not find them. The next morning, letting his sheep out to pasture, the cyclops rolled the giant rock door partly open. As each animal left the cave, Polyphemus felt its back, making sure no Greek was riding atop a sheep. But clever Ulysses had strapped each man to the belly of a sheep, tricking Polyphemus, who felt only the backs of the animals as they passed by. Finally, Ulysses himself escaped, holding onto the thick woolly underbelly of the last sheep.

As the Greeks quickly set sail, Ulysses called out to the cyclops, "To all who ask, tell them Ulysses has done this to you." In his pride, however, Ulysses unknowingly contributed to the tragic events that lay ahead on his journey. Polyphemus prayed to his father Poseidon to punish Ulysses, and the sea god did just that.

11. Ulysses and the island of cannibals.

Before long, Ulysses and his men rejoined the rest of the fleet and continued their journey back to Ithaca. After a time, the ships encountered another island with a sheltered harbor ringed by high cliffs. Eleven ships of the fleet entered the cove and anchored. Because there was no more room in the harbor, Ulysses' ship anchored just outside the mouth of the inlet.

When several crewmen went ashore to look for food and water, they wandered into a village of giants. Without warning, Antiphates, king of the giants, grabbed several men and began to eat them alive! Running for their lives, Ulysses' men quickly boarded their ships, but the cannibals rained down huge rocks and spears on the trapped vessels. All eleven ships were destroyed and their crews killed. Only Ulysses and his crew survived, sailing away on their ship that had been moored safely outside the harbor.

12. Ulysses and Circe.

Continuing to sail northwest, Ulysses' ship made landfall on the island-home of Circe, the enchantress. Welcoming Ulysses and his men, she had a feast prepared for them. The hungry sailors greedily devoured the food and drank much wine. Soon they were behaving like a crude, drunken mob. Offended by this behavior, which reminded her of the actions of pigs, the enchantress used her magic to transform the crewmen into those very animals.

Eventually Circe turned the men back into human beings, and she and Ulysses became lovers. After a year of living in peace and luxury, Ulysses knew in his heart that he must return to his beloved Penelope. Circe also realized that Ulysses had to leave and sadly bade him farewell. Before he departed, she advised him to go to the Land of the Dead and consult with the ghost of the blind prophet Tiresias.

13. Ulysses and the sirens.

Circe had warned Ulysses that he would pass the Island of the Sirens on his journey. These beautiful creatures, part woman and part bird, sang sweet songs that drew sailors toward the island until their ships crashed into the dangerous rocks along the coast. As his ship neared the sirens' island, Ulysses instructed his men to plug their ears with beeswax so they couldn't hear the sweet but deadly singing. He also ordered his men to tie him securely to the mast, and told them that when the time came, they were to resist his pleas to go toward the sirens.

The strategy worked and the ship sailed quickly past the treacherous creatures and their deadly island.

After many days, Ulysses' ship reached the Land of the Dead. Wandering among the frightening spirits and shades, he finally found the ghost of Tiresias. The blind prophet warned Ulysses that the sea god Poseidon was seeking revenge upon him for blinding his son Polyphemus. Shaken by his visit to the underworld, Ulysses quickly set sail with his men.

Spain

Corsica

Island of
Cannibals

Circe's
Island

Italy

Adriatic Sea

Sardinia

Sirens

Aeolus

Phaeacia
Princess
Nausicaa

Ithaca

Jonian
Sea

Cyclops

Sicily

Scylla and
Charybdis

Calypso's
Island

Land of
the Dead

Tunisia

Malta

Island of
Lotus Eaters

14.–15. The World of Ulysses.

Over the years, many scholars and historians have tried to locate and identify the actual geographical locations mentioned in the *Iliad* and the *Odyssey*.

The fabled city of Troy itself was finally found to have actually existed on the coast of modern-day Turkey. Discovered in 1870 by German archaeologist

The World of Ulysses

Black Sea

Land of the Hittites
(Turkey)

Troy

Aegean
Sea

Rhodes

Syria

Cyprus

Crete

Mediterranean Sea

Arabia

Egypt

ya

Red Sea

Heinrich Schliemann, and since excavated by many other archaeologists, the ruins revealed that Troy was just one of nine cities that had existed on the same site. The map above shows one version of possible locations for the various adventures of Ulysses.

16.–17. Ulysses encounters Scylla and Charybdis.

Among the dangers faced by Ulysses and his men on their voyage back to Ithaca were the sea monster Scylla, and the whirlpool Charybdis. They guarded a narrow channel of water through which the ship had to pass. Scylla was a creature with six snake-like heads filled with sharp teeth. The beast could whip its heads out at lightning speed, snatching and devouring sailors off ships sailing through the channel. If a ship were to steer away from the monster

it then faced the whirlpool Charybdis, a boiling, churning vortex of water able to suck any ship down into the ocean depths. Ulysses gave strict orders to the crew to be on the lookout for these two threats. In spite of their caution, however, disaster struck. Sailing close to the side of the channel near the sea monster in order to avoid the whirlpool, Ulysses lost six brave crewmen to the monster's jaws before escaping back into the open sea.

18. Zeus destroys Ulysses' ship.

Ulysses had been warned by the ghost of Tiresias to avoid the island of Helios, the sun god. But after many days at sea, the hungry crew persuaded their captain to land on the island for rest, food, and water. Ulysses strictly forbade his men from slaughtering and eating any of the sun god's sacred cattle grazing on the island. Unfortunately, the starving crew could not resist, killing and roasting several of the sacred creatures. Furious that his cattle had been eaten, Helios called on Zeus to punish Ulysses and his men for their offense. In response, Zeus sent powerful lightning bolts that shattered Ulysses' ship. The only survivor was Ulysses himself, left floating in the open sea on a piece of wooden wreckage.

19. Penelope and her suitors.

All during the years of the Trojan War and Ulysses' long journey home, his faithful and loving wife Penelope awaited his return. Some of the noblemen of the kingdom, however, were convinced that Ulysses was dead and that Penelope should marry one of them. These aggressive suitors besieged her with demands to choose a new husband who would then claim the throne of Ithaca.

They finally moved into the royal palace, eating, drinking, and abusing Penelope's dignity and honor. They also plotted the murder of Ulysses' son Telemachus, now a young man. Penelope was in a desperate situation, but with a cleverness worthy of Ulysses himself, she formulated a plan to keep her suitors at bay.

20. Penelope outwits her belligerent suitors.

In response to the demands of her suitors that she choose a new husband, Penelope agreed to make a decision after she completed weaving the shroud (burial cloth) of old King Laertes, who was close to death. During the day she worked on the weaving, but at night, she secretly unraveled most of the day's work. In this way she was able to delay her decision for three more years as the suitors waited for her to finish the last stitch. Finally, she was betrayed by one of her maids, who told the suitors of her deception. Angry and hostile, they confronted Penelope and insisted she make a decision. Unbeknownst to her and them, however, Ulysses was slowly making his way ever closer to Ithaca.

21. Ulysses on the island of Calypso.

After his ship and crew were destroyed by Zeus, Ulysses eventually washed ashore on a lush island, home of the nymph Calypso. Calypso nursed and cared for Ulysses, and the two grew very fond of each other. In fact, Ulysses stayed with Calypso for several years. But finally the pull of Penelope's love and his homesickness for Ithaca became too great. Ulysses wanted to leave the island, much to the dismay of Calypso, who forbade him to build a raft. The goddess Athena, however, Ulysses' guide and protector, took pity on him and sent Hermes, messenger of the gods, to persuade Calypso to let Ulysses leave. Reluctantly, Calypso relented. She watched as Ulysses built a raft, and sadly bade him farewell.

22. Poseidon destroys the raft of Ulysses.

Ulysses sailed for seventeen days on his handbuilt raft. On the eighteenth day, running low on food and water, he was fortunate to sight land in the distance. But cruel Poseidon saw an opportunity to take revenge on Ulysses. He called up a great storm with waves so high and pow-erful that they smashed Ulysses' raft. Clinging to a piece of his shattered vessel, the Greek warrior mustered all his remaining strength and determination and swam toward the distant shore.

23. Ulysses meets Princess Nausicaa and King Alcinous.

Ulysses finally washed ashore on the beach, exhausted, covered in seaweed and wooden wreckage. In the distance, some young women were playing ball. Their leader, Princess Nausicaa of Phaeacia, approached the half-drowned stranger.

Ulysses told her of all the dangers and travails he had endured on his journey. Taking pity on him, Nausicaa brought Ulysses to the royal palace, fed and clothed him, and presented him to her father, King Alcinous. Impressed by the tale of Ulysses' odyssey, the king ordered a ship and fifty rowers to transport the hero back to his homeland. Anchoring at night in one of the bays of Ithaca, the rowers carried the sleeping Ulysses ashore, gently placing him on the beach.

24. Ulysses is disguised by the goddess Athena.

When Ulysses awoke he was disoriented and confused. Walking inland, he encountered an aged shepherd, who was suddenly transformed into the beautiful goddess Athena. She told him that he was finally home but that his throne, his wife Penelope, and his son Telemachus were in danger from the queen's belligerent suitors.

To help Ulysses recover his kingdom and avenge the disrespect shown to Penelope, Athena magically changed his appearance to that of a withered old beggar. Disguised, he would be better able to form a plan to save Penelope and Telemachus. Ulysses then encountered a young man who asked him where he had come from. At that moment Athena whispered in Ulysses' ear, "This is Telemachus, your son, now grown into a young man." Weeping with happiness, Ulysses revealed to Telemachus that he was none other than his father, finally returned after a twenty-year odyssey. Father and son embraced joyfully, then began to plan their revenge.

25. Ulysses arrives at his palace.

Ulysses reached his palace still disguised as a beggar. Although the suitors, gathered in the great hall for a feast, insulted and derided him, Penelope took pity on the old man clothed in rags. She ordered her servant, Eurycleia, to bathe his feet and give him some food and wine. Eurycleia had been Ulysses' nursemaid when he was an infant and young boy and loved him dearly. As she began to bathe his feet she noticed the telltale scar above Ulysses' knee and immediately knew he had returned in disguise. Seeing signs of recognition in her face, Ulysses cautioned Eurycleia to keep silent about his true identity until his plan was ready.

26.–27. Ulysses reveals himself.

At the feast, Penelope's suitors demanded she finally choose one of them as her new husband. She replied that she would marry whoever could string Ulysses' mighty bow and shoot an arrow through twelve axeheads set up in the hall. One by one, the suitors wrestled with the powerful bow but failed to bend and string it.

The angry suitors protested to Penelope that the test was unfair and that she should choose a husband by some other means. Before she could answer, the old beggar stood up and quietly asked if he could try to string the bow. The suitors laughed and jeered at the old man, but Penelope gave her permission to the ragged stranger.

At first, the beggar struggled with the bow, seemingly unable to accomplish the feat, but suddenly he bent and strung the weapon with ease. Quickly nocking an arrow, he shot it cleanly through all twelve axeheads. As the suitors stared in disbelief, the beggar was revealed by Athena as none other than Ulysses.

"The contest is over, now begins the dancing!" shouted Ulysses. This was the signal for he and Telemachus to begin the battle with the suitors. As the conflict was joined, Ulysses took his revenge, sending arrows from his bow to their targets with lightning speed and accuracy.

28. Ulysses and Telemachus battle Penelope's suitors.

First with arrows and spears, then with swords and daggers, Ulysses and Telemachus fought the battle in the great hall. Enraged by the suitors' abuse of his queen, Ulysses killed one after another. Soon the great hall was awash in blood and strewn with the bodies of Penelope's tormentors.

Eurycleia ran to tell her mistress of the return of Ulysses and his revenge on her behalf. Stunned, Penelope entered the hall and looked at Ulysses, now resting upon his throne. At first, she was not sure it was her beloved husband—gone for so many years, but now sitting before her. To reassure her, Ulysses spoke to her of the bed he had carved for them from a living olive tree twenty long years ago. No one else knew of the bed. All doubt was erased as husband and wife rushed to embrace one another.

29. Athena makes peace on Ithaca.

Peace in Ulysses' kingdom was not yet at hand, however. The relatives of Penelope's suitors had armed themselves and were approaching the palace, driven by thoughts of revenge for the suitors' deaths. Ulysses, Telemachus, and the servants of the household gathered weapons to meet the angry mob. As they were about to clash, the goddess Athena appeared, bathed in a golden light. "Drop your weapons, there has been enough killing!" she cried out to them. In awe of the great goddess, both sides agreed to make peace.

As a result, Ulysses and his beloved Penelope were able to live out the rest of their lives in serenity and contentment. Centuries later, the story of the great Trojan War and Ulysses' remarkable odyssey back to his homeland were immortalized by Homer, and became part of the myth and legend of Western civilization.